A-Z of
Animal Jokes

A-Z of
Animal Jokes

Scoular Anderson

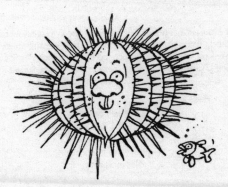

CORGI BOOKS

A-Z OF ANIMAL JOKES
A CORGI BOOK 978 0 552 56334 5

Published by Corgi,
An imprint of Random House Children's Books
A Random House Group Company

First published by Corgi in 1987
This edition published 2010

1 3 5 7 9 10 8 6 4 2

Text and illustrations © Scoular Anderson 1987

The right of Scoular Anderson to be identified as the author and illustrator of
this work has been asserted in accordance with the Copyright, Designs and
Patents Act 1988.

The Random House Group Limited supports the Forest Stewardship Council
(FSC), the leading international forest certification organization. All our titles
that are printed on Greenpeace-approved FSC-certified paper carry the FSC
logo. Our paper procurement policy can be found at
www.rbooks.co.uk/environment.

Mixed Sources
Product group from well-managed
forests and other controlled sources
www.fsc.org Cert no. TT-COC-2139
© 1996 Forest Stewardship Council
FSC

Set in Sabon

Corgi Books are published by Random House Children's Books,
61-63 Uxbridge Road, London W5 5SA

www.kidsatrandomhouse.co.uk
www.rbooks.co.uk

Addresses for companies within The Random House Group Limited can be
found at: www.randomhouse.co.uk/offices.htm

THE RANDOM HOUSE GROUP Limited Reg. No. 954009

A CIP catalogue record for this book is available from the British Library.

Printed in the UK by CPI Bookmarque, Croydon, CR0 4TD

For Lorn and Camille

COME ON,
WE'VE GOT
WORK TO
DO!

At his party the zebra threw buns,
And popped corks from a small plastic gun.
Then just for a wheeze,
He shot the aardvark with peas
– But the aardvark has no sense of fun.

The angora goat's very hairy,
So you must be exceedingly wary,
For when the wind blows,
The fluff tickles his nose,
And his sneezing becomes almost scary.

Where do baby chimpanzees sleep?
In an apricot.

What are the largest ants in the world?
Elephants.

Knock Knock.
Who's there?
Thea.
Thea who?
Thea later alligator.

11

A boa with coils uneven,
Has the greatest trouble in breathin'.
With jokes she's afflicted,
For her laughs get constricted,
And her coils start writhin' and wreathin'.

What did the beaver say to the tree?
It's been nice gnawing you!

Why wouldn't they let
the butterfly into the dance?
Because it was a moth ball.

ANYONE WANT
TO LEARN THE
JITTERBUG?

Have you heard about the boy who does
bird impressions?
He eats worms.

A chameleon's skin changes its hue,
To match the jungle that it passes
                        through.
If it strayed from a kilt
To a pink patchwork quilt,
Would it stripe itself green, pink
                        and blue?

HELP!

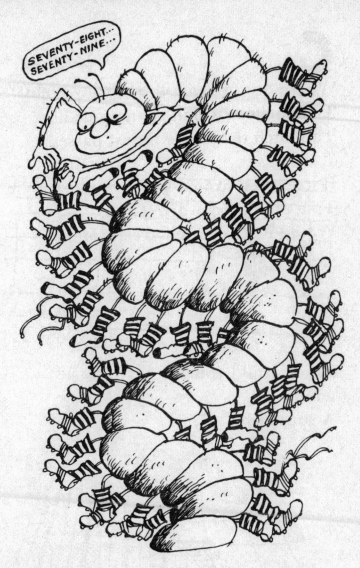

Why did the insects drop the centipede
from their football team?
He took too long to put his boots on.

Where do cows go on Saturday nights?
To the moovies.

What would your cat be if she ate a
lemon?
A sourpuss.

Where do giant condors come from?
Eggs.

WHAT DO YOU CALL A DAIRYMAN FRIGHTENED OF MILKING?

A COWARD

On an island men came to explore,
They found dodos were crowding the
                            shore.
When the men brought out rifles,
The birds laughed at such trifles,
And now the poor dodo's no more.

Knock knock.
Who's there?
Dinah.
Dinah who?
Dinosaurus through the letterbox.

What did the donkey say when he had only thistles to eat?

A schoolboy put – just for a jest –
A soccer ball in an emu's nest.
When the family appeared,
It looked rather weird –
Six chicks and a striped football vest.

WHAT A LAUGH!

What did the earwig say as he fell?

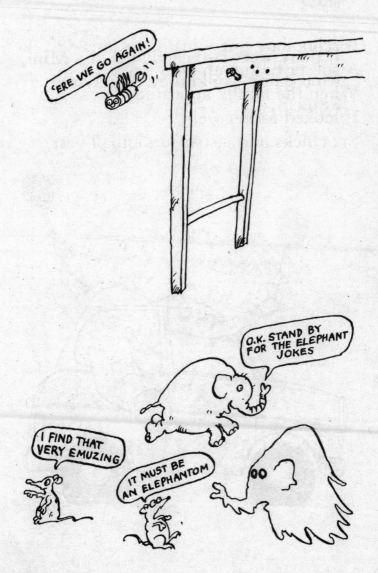

If there were two elephants in a Mini,
what game would they be playing?
Squash.

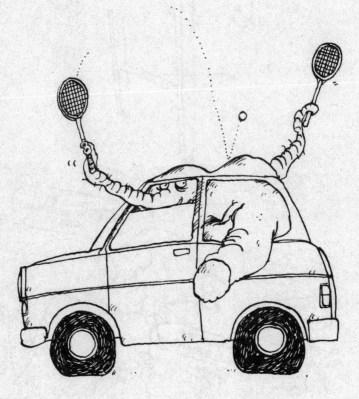

When do elephants have eight feet?
When there are two of them.

There once was a man called MacGringo,
Who thought he'd get rich playing bingo.
While others got prizes
Of fabulous sizes,
All he won was a plastic flamingo.

Why did the fly fly?
Because the spider spied 'er.

What's the difference between a flea
and a coyote?
**One prowls on the hairy, the other
howls on the prairie.**

When is a car like a frog?
When it's being toad.

How do you write a letter to a fish?
Drop it a line.

While playing party games, a young gnat,
Decided to hide in a hat,
But an elderly guest,
Decided to rest,
Now the gnat and the hat are quite flat.

Where do monkeys make toast?
Under the gorilla.

What kind of gulls eat rabbits?
Eagulls.

A haddock who built model ships,
By chopping up wood into strips,
One day found a flaw,
In his motorized saw,
And now he's just haddock and chips.

What do you call a laughing hippo?
A happypotamus.

What is a horse's favourite game?
Stable tennis.

An ibex with horns spectacular,
Whose curves were impressively circular,
Once charged at a log,
Which he thought was a dog,
Now his horns are strangely triangular.

Waiter, there's an insect in my soup!
**What do you expect for 20p – an
elephant?**

There once was a dashing young jellyfish,
Who married a sweet young shellyfish.
They both had the notion,
To dance round the ocean,
And became better known as the jollyfish.

What do you get if you cross an elephant
with a hose?
A jumbo jet.

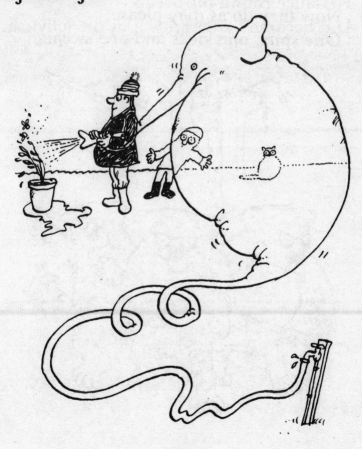

It's a terrible state of affairs,
But a group of young koala bears,
Once lived quietly in trees,
Now they do as they please,
One spits, one kicks and one swears.

What kind of cat drives an ambulance?
A first-aid kit.

What kind of bird unlocks doors?
A kiwi.

What happens when you cross a sheep
with a kangaroo?
You get a woolly jumper.

A sly old beast is the lynx,
She smiles and gives friendly wynx,
But she only pretends
To make good friends,
She'll eat you before you can blynx.

49

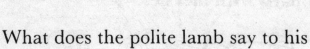

What does the polite lamb say to his mother?

What's yellow and covered in black and red spots?
A leopard with measles.

An inquisitive moose strayed too near
An adventurous young pioneer,
So this gigantic beast,
Made a wonderful feast,
And his antlers a fine chandelier.

What is the biggest moth in the world?
The mammoth.

What do you call a mouse that can pick up an elephant?
Sir.

What do you call a Scottish parrot?
A Macaw.

How do you stop a mole digging in your garden?
Hide his spade.

There was a great Nile crocodile,
Who would rarely break out in a smile,
For his fondness of sweets,
And other such treats,
Made his jaws look exceedingly vile.

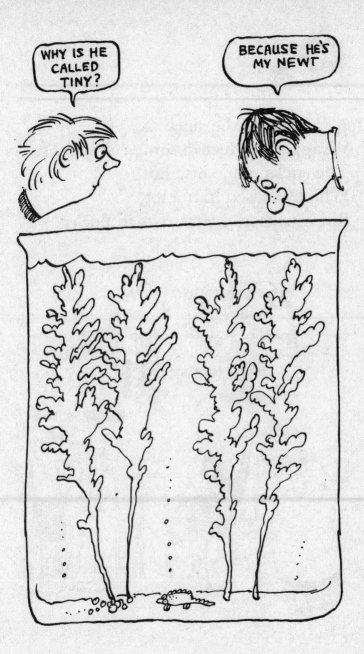

A chilly old Aberdeen ox
Wrapped his feet in some colourful socks.
The socks made him hot,
Which pleased him a lot,
But attracted the tourists in flocks.

Why did the owl 'owl?
Because the woodpecker would peck 'er.

What animal is it best to be on a cold day?
A little otter.

Thought panda: 'I'm very aware
I'm a bear who is handsome yet rare,
But have I green scales?
Red eyeballs? Blue nails?
For humans just stand there and stare.'

What did the baby porcupine say when
he backed into a cactus?
Is that you, Ma?

What goes up the river at 100 kilometres an hour?
A motor pike.

Where do zoo birds keep their food?
In pelicans.

Why did the farmer call his pig Ink?
Because it kept running out of the pen.

A quail who o'erheard a complaint,
That her feathers looked spotted with
paint,
Spent a day getting clean
In a washing machine,
But ended up queasy and faint.

What kind of doctor treats a duck?
A quack doctor.

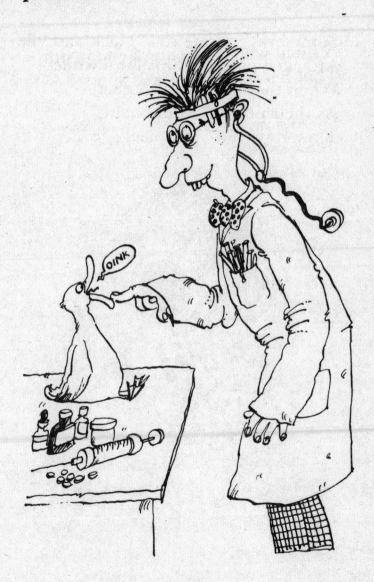

Some brave pirate rats, black and vile,
Attacked passing ships for a while.
When they got as much gold
As their pockets would hold,
They retired to a tropical isle.

LITTLE
BRAT

Why did the bald man put rabbits on his head?
Because from the distance they would look like hares.

Why did the rooster refuse to fight?
Because he was chicken.

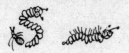

A musical squid learned the flute,
And could rattle a drum with one foot.
Then he practised all day
And was able to play
The piano, guitar and the lute.

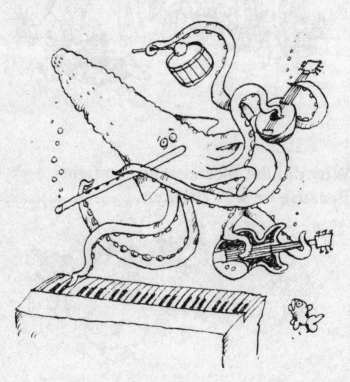

Child: Daddy, there's a spider in the bath!

Father: Don't worry, you've seen spiders before.

Child: But this one's three metres wide and is using all the hot water!

What animals use nutcrackers?
Toothless squirrels.

Did you hear about the sheepdog trials?
Two of the dogs were found guilty.

A toucan made other birds shriek
By tweaking their toes with her beak.
She once bit the claws
Of a bird with huge jaws,
And tweaked nothing more for a week.

What do you call a tyrannosaurus with earphones on?
Anything you like because he can't hear you.

What fish sings songs?
A tuna fish.

Where do tadpoles change into frogs?
In the croakroom.

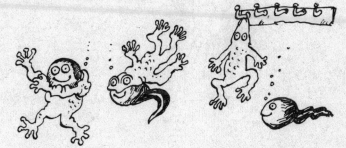

An ugly sea urchin called Archy,
Had spines that were specially scratchy,
But much to his anguish,
A spine-nibbling cat fish,
Made Archy look peevish and patchy.

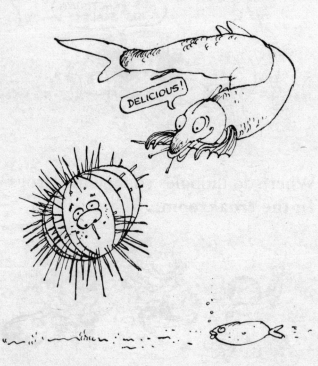

What animals wear badly fitting shoes?
Unicorns.

A vulture was invited to dine
By his charmingly sweet valentine,
But when he got there,
He found that the fare
Was pineapple dumpling with wine.

What snakes are found on cars?
Windscreen vipers.

Why are vampires crazy?
Because they are often bats.

A warthog who thought herself plain,
Tried to dress herself up, but in vain,
For her ringlets and spangles,
And an earring which dangles,
Have been utterly ruined by rain.

Knock knock.
Who's there?
Weevil.
Weevil who?
Weevil make you talk!

Where would you weigh a whale?
At a whale-weigh station.

Xiphias, as everyone knows,
Is a fish with a sword-like nose.
If other fish sneer,
He fills them with fear,
By using his nose to strike blows.

The Yapok, like beaver and otter,
Goes swimming about in the water.
His song, loud and shrill,
Can be heard in Brazil,
Where the water is definitely hotter.

What animal gossips most?
The yak.

The zebra dressed up as a sheep,
And danced till he fell in a heap.
Would the aardvark not smile,
Just once in a while?
But the aardvark fell quietly asleep.

What's black and white and noisy?
A zebra with a set of drums.

A beast in a black and white suit,
Would caper around me and hoot.
He stood on his head
Until he went red,
While wearing a hat on one foot.

His eyes had a terrible gleam,
And his ears were gushing with steam,
As he danced several hornpipes
While playing the bagpipes –
Could all this have been a bad dream?